SPORTS SUPERSTARS

JUSTIN JEFFERSON

BY THOMAS K. ADAMSON

TORQUE™

BELLWETHER MEDIA·MINNEAPOLIS, MN

Torque brims with excitement perfect for thrill-seekers of all kinds. Discover daring survival skills, explore uncharted worlds, and marvel at mighty engines and extreme sports. In *Torque* books, anything can happen. Are you ready?

This edition first published in 2025 by Bellwether Media, Inc.

No part of this publication may be reproduced in whole or in part without written permission of the publisher. For information regarding permission, write to Bellwether Media, Inc., Attention: Permissions Department, 6012 Blue Circle Drive, Minnetonka, MN 55343.

Library of Congress Cataloging-in-Publication Data

Names: Adamson, Thomas K., 1970- author.
Title: Justin Jefferson / by Thomas K. Adamson.
Description: Minneapolis, MN : Bellwether Media, 2025. | Series: Torque. Sports superstars | Includes bibliographical references and index. | Audience: Ages 7-12 | Audience: Grades 4-6 | Summary: "Engaging images accompany information about Justin Jefferson. The combination of high-interest subject matter and light text is intended for students in grades 3 through 7– Provided by publisher.
Identifiers: LCCN 2024009923 (print) | LCCN 2024009924 (ebook) | ISBN 9798893040340 (library binding) | ISBN 9781644879702 (ebook)
Subjects: LCSH: Jefferson, Justin, 1999–Juvenile literature. | Wide receivers (Football)–Biography–Juvenile literature. | Football players–United States–Biography–Juvenile literature.
Classification: LCC GV939.J44 A73 2025 (print) | LCC GV939.J44 (ebook)
LC record available at https://lccn.loc.gov/2024009923
LC ebook record available at https://lccn.loc.gov/2024009924

Text copyright © 2025 by Bellwether Media, Inc. TORQUE and associated logos are trademarks and/or registered trademarks of Bellwether Media, Inc. Bellwether Media is a division of Chrysalis Education Group.

Editor: Kieran Downs   Designer: Gabriel Hilger

Printed in the United States of America, North Mankato, MN.

TABLE OF CONTENTS

THE CATCH OF HIS LIFE	4
WHO IS JUSTIN JEFFERSON?	6
COLLEGE CHAMPIONSHIP	8
AN EARLY STAR	12
JEFFERSON'S FUTURE	20
GLOSSARY	22
TO LEARN MORE	23
INDEX	24

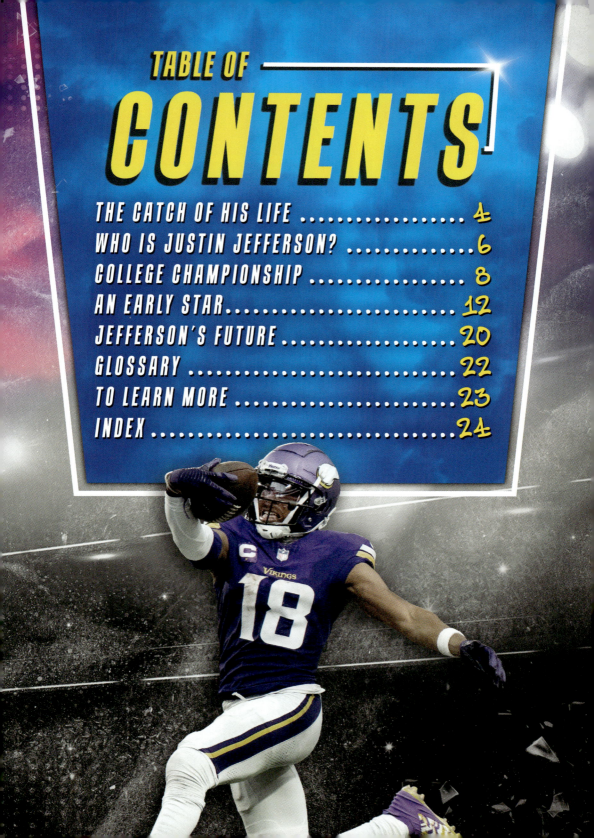

THE CATCH OF HIS LIFE

The Vikings trail the Bills by four points. It is fourth down. Kirk Cousins tosses the ball to Justin Jefferson. The pass is high. Jefferson leaps, reaching backward.

The Bills **defender** seems to have the ball. But Jefferson's right hand holds the ball as he lands on his back. First down Vikings! They go on to get a comeback win!

Best Play Award

Jefferson's catch won the ESPN ESPY award for best play of 2022.

WHO IS JUSTIN JEFFERSON?

Justin Jefferson is a **wide receiver** in the **National Football League** (NFL). He uses his quickness to get open for passes. He makes impossible catches and big plays.

JETS
JEFFERSON'S NICKNAME IS JETS.

JUSTIN JEFFERSON

BIRTHDAY	June 16, 1999
HOMETOWN	St. Rose, Louisiana
POSITION	wide receiver
HEIGHT	6 feet 1 inch
DRAFTED	Minnesota Vikings in the 1st round (22nd overall) of the 2020 NFL Draft

Jefferson also started a dance craze with the Griddy **touchdown** celebration. He started doing it in college. He even uses different kinds of the Griddy.

COLLEGE CHAMPIONSHIP

Jefferson was always playing football with his two older brothers growing up. His brothers said they never went easy on him.

JEFFERSON WITH HIS BROTHER

LOUISIANA STATE UNIVERSITY

Jefferson played both **offense** and defense for his high school football team. He was also great at track and field. His brothers played football at Louisiana State University (LSU). So Jefferson went there, too.

As a first-year, Jefferson rarely played. He did not catch any passes. But he was a big part of LSU's offense in 2018.

In 2019, Jefferson broke a school record by catching 111 passes. He gained 1,540 yards and scored 18 touchdowns. He helped LSU win the National **Championship**. He caught 9 passes for 106 yards in the game.

2019 NATIONAL CHAMPIONSHIP

Great Pass Catchers

In 2019, Jefferson and teammate Ja'Marr Chase were the best wide receiver team in college football. They combined for 3,320 yards and 38 touchdowns.

AN EARLY STAR

In 2020, the Minnesota Vikings **drafted** Jefferson in the first round. Coaches liked how hard he worked during practice.

In the first NFL game he started, Jefferson had seven catches for 175 yards. After gaining 1,400 receiving yards as a **rookie**, Jefferson was named to the 2020 All-Rookie Team. He also made the **Pro Bowl** that season.

FAVORITES

MUSIC   **HOBBY**   **COOKIE**   **ICE CREAM**

Lil Wayne   video games   white chocolate macadamia   vanilla caramel

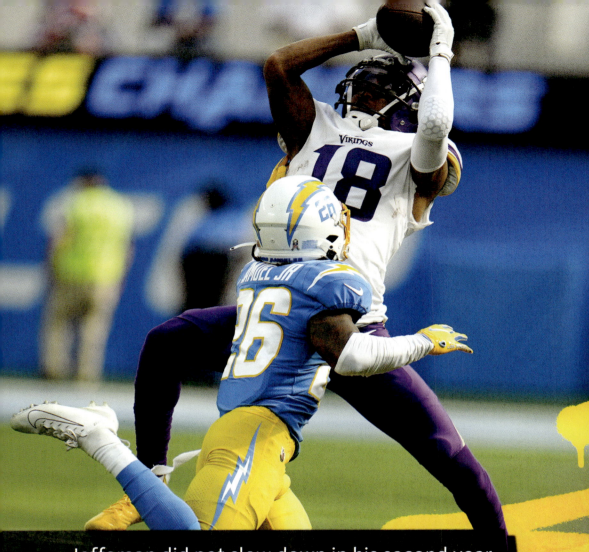

Jefferson did not slow down in his second year. He gained 1,616 receiving yards. He was the first player to gain 3,000 receiving yards in his first two NFL seasons.

For the second year in a row, he was a second team **All-Pro**. He was also named to his second Pro Bowl.

In 2022, Jefferson was impossible to stop. He led the NFL with 128 catches for 1,809 yards. He had many big plays.

He helped the Vikings reach the **playoffs**. He was named the 2022 Offensive Player of the Year. He was also a first team All-Pro for the first time.

Jefferson started the 2023 season strong. But he got hurt in the fifth game. He missed seven games. But he still gained over 1,000 yards for the season.

He set an NFL record for the most receiving yards in a player's first four seasons. After the 2023 season, he had 5,899 yards in just 60 games.

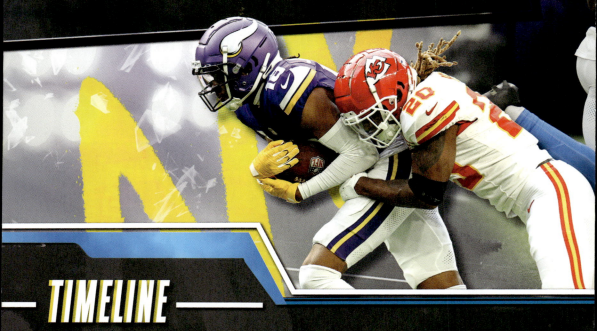

TIMELINE

— 2017 —
Jefferson joins the LSU football team

— 2019 —
Jefferson wins the National Championship with LSU

18

Fast Track

Jefferson reached 5,000 receiving yards in the fewest games of any NFL player.

— 2020 —
Jefferson is drafted by the Vikings

— 2022 —
Jefferson is named the Offensive Player of the Year

— 2023 —
Jefferson reaches 5,000 receiving yards

JEFFERSON'S FUTURE

Jefferson works to promote flag football around the world. He wants kids to see how much fun the sport is. He also wants them to know that everyone can play. He has also supported programs that help kids in need finish school.

Jefferson always works to learn more and get even better. He wants to break more records!

21

GLOSSARY

All-Pro—an honor for football players who are the best at each position during a season

championship—a contest to decide the best team or person

defender—a player who tries to stop the opposing team from scoring

drafted—chose by a process where professional teams choose high school and college athletes to play for them

National Football League—a professional football league in the United States; the National Football League is often called the NFL.

offense—players who have the ball and are trying to score

playoffs—games played after the regular season is over; playoff games determine which teams play in the championship game.

Pro Bowl—a game between the best players in the NFL

rookie—a first-year player in a sports league

touchdown—a score that occurs when a team crosses into their opponent's end zone with the football; a touchdown is worth six points.

wide receiver—a player on offense whose main job is to catch passes from the quarterback

TO LEARN MORE

AT THE LIBRARY

Downs, Kieran. *The Minnesota Vikings*. Minneapolis, Minn.: Bellwether Media, 2024.

Gigliotti, Jim. *Justin Jefferson vs. Randy Moss: Who Would Win?* Minneapolis, Minn.: Lerner Publications, 2025.

Smith, Elliott. *Meet Justin Jefferson: Minnesota Vikings Superstar*. Minneapolis, Minn.: Lerner Publications, 2024.

ON THE WEB

FACTSURFER

Factsurfer.com gives you a safe, fun way to find more information.

1. Go to www.factsurfer.com

2. Enter "Justin Jefferson" into the search box and click 🔍.

3. Select your book cover to see a list of related content.

INDEX

All-Pro, 14, 16
All-Rookie Team, 12
awards, 5, 16, 17
catches, 4, 5, 6, 10, 11, 12, 16
championship, 11
childhood, 8, 9
defender, 4
defense, 9
drafted, 12
family, 8, 9
favorites, 13
flag football, 20
future, 21
Griddy, 7
hurt, 18
Louisiana State University, 7, 9, 10, 11
map, 15
Minnesota Vikings, 4, 12, 16
National Football League, 6, 12, 14, 16, 18, 19
nickname, 6
offense, 9, 10
Offensive Player of the Year, 16, 17
playoffs, 16
Pro Bowl, 12, 14, 15
profile, 7
records, 11, 14, 18, 19, 21
timeline, 18–19
touchdown, 7, 11
trophy shelf, 17
wide receiver, 6, 11
yards, 11, 12, 14, 16, 18, 19

The images in this book are reproduced through the courtesy of: Nick Wosika/ AP Images, front cover; Jerry Holt/ AP Images, p. 3; Joshua Bessex/ AP Images, p. 4; Isaiah Vazquez/ Stringer/ Getty, pp. 4-5; G. Newman Lowrance/ AP Images, p. 6; Karen Hovsepyan/ Alamy, p. 7 (VIkings Logo); Stacy Bengs/ AP Images, p. 7 (Justin Jefferson); Celso Pupo, p. 8; Chad Robertson Media, p. 9; Zuma Press, Inc./ Alamy, p. 10; Todd Kirkland/ Icon Sportswire/ AP Images, p. 11; Jim Mone/ AP Images, p. 12; David Berding/ AP Images, p. 13 (Justin Jefferson); Steve Sykes, p. 13 (Lil Wayne); Diego Thomazini, p. 13 (video games); Tiger Images, p. 13 (white chocolate macadamia); Stephanie Frey, p. 13 (vanilla caramel); Gregory Bull/ AP Images, p. 14; Photo Image, p. 15 (U.S. Bank Stadium); David Becker/ AP Images, p. 15 (2021 Pro Bowl); Abbie Parr/ AP Images, p. 16; Ross D. Franklin/ AP Images, p. 17; LSU/ Wikipedia, p. 18 (LSU Logo); Kansas City Chief/ AP Images, p. 18 (Justin Jefferson); Joe Robbins/ AP Images, pp. 18-19; Minnesota Vikings/ Wikipedia, p. 19 (Vikings Logo); David J. Phillip, p. 19 (2022); Bruce Kluckhohn/ AP Images, p. 20; Ryan Kang/ AP Images, p. 21.